*L*OOKING AT *P*AINTINGS

Cats

Detail from *Studies of a Cat from Kuniyoshi's Sketchbook*
Utagawa Kuniyoshi, Japanese (1797–1861)

LOOKING AT PAINTINGS

Cats

Peggy Roalf

Series Editor
Jacques Lowe

Designer
Amy Hill

Hyperion Books for Children

A
JACQUES LOWE
VISUAL ARTS PROJECTS
BOOK

Text Copyright © 1992 by Jacques Lowe Visual Arts Projects Inc.
A Jacques Lowe Visual Arts Projects Book

Printed in Italy

FIRST EDITION

1 3 5 7 9 10 8 6 4 2

ISBN: 1-56282-091-5 (trade)
ISBN: 1-56282-092-3 (lib. bdg.)

LC# 91-73829

Contents

For Kate Kreminski,
with love

Introduction

*L*OOKING AT PAINTINGS is a series of books about understanding what great artists see when they paint. Five thousand years ago, the ancient Egyptians worshiped the cat as a god. Since that time, painters have been fascinated by the mysterious qualities of this animal—its keen vision, skill as a hunter, and fierce independence; its cleanliness and graceful form; its aloofness and its affection for people. Some artists have created images of cats to signify heroic or destructive historical figures. Others have captured the graceful charm or sly humor of a cherished family pet.

In many cultures, the cat has been a symbol of fertility, motherhood, and good harvests. But in medieval Europe, cats were believed to be demons, and hundreds of thousands were burned to death. By looking at many paintings of cats, we can see how painters have conveyed their own feelings about these animals—with the same attention they have given to their human subjects.

A self-taught American artist painted *Tinkle, a Cat* as a feline princess, using rich colors to create the life-size portrait of a beloved pet. In *Paris Through the Window*, Marc Chagall created a mysterious cat with a human face as one of several imaginary figures, to convey the happiness he felt when he achieved his first artistic success. In *Cat Seizing Bird*, Pablo Picasso symbolized the destructive force of a mad dictator as a predatory cat—and created a powerful image warning of the terrible times ahead for the world.

Artists have transformed their vision of cats into images of fantasy, images of power, and images of happiness. You can learn to observe the personality of your cat—and with your imagination, picture your pet with the eyes of a painter.

THE SUN GOD RA IN THE FORM OF A CAT, about 1300 B.C.
Facsimile of Egyptian wall painting, 19th Dynasty, Gouache on paper, 33^1/$_4$" x 18^1/$_2$"

In ancient Egypt, cats were treasured as household pets and as symbols of fertility. Like their human companions, deceased cats were mummified and placed in a tomb to await the next life. These elaborate tombs were decorated with murals that often featured images of cats as playmates and as protectors.

One of the most important Egyptian deities was the sun god Ra, portrayed as a cat because of that animal's ability to see in the dark. In this painting, Ra defeats Apophis, the god of darkness, who takes the form of a great serpent. Using only four colors—black, white, yellow, and green—the painter created a powerful image with bold forms. Fluid black outlines define the cat's regal posture, swept-back ears, and large, all-seeing eye. Ra's golden coloring is the same as the background, but the expressive gray and white markings create the appearance of another shade of yellow. The artist painted the snake's silvery-looking skin by applying a thin layer of white paint on top of a black silhouette. The thick black outlines and gray spots form a bold contrast to the pale background.

The original of this painting was created about three thousand years ago. Since then, the picture has been damaged—by time and by vandals. In 1910, the Metropolitan Museum of Art in New York sent an expedition of archeologists to study the ancient tombs of Thebes. The artist Charles K. Wilkinson spent twelve years in Egypt creating *facsimile paintings*—exact, full-size copies of the wall paintings—which archeologists have studied to understand the daily life and culture of a vanished Egyptian civilization.

Like most fifteenth-century artists, Leonardo da Vinci created religious paintings for churches. In this portrait, Leonardo painted the Madonna and child as ordinary people with their pet cat. The dark shadows behind the figures focus our attention on the mother, the child, and the cat.

ANNUNCIATION, Detail, 1528
Lorenzo Lotto, Italian (about 1480–1556), Oil on canvas, 63⅜″ x 44⅞″

The Italian Renaissance was an era that produced great advances in painting. Fifteenth-century artists had developed the method of *perspective drawing* to shape the appearance of three-dimensional space. Refinement of the oil painting technique enabled artists to create colors and forms that had never before been possible. It almost seemed that the art of painting had been perfected.

Lotto made the floor appear to slant dangerously forward, spilling the room out toward the viewer, to intensify the drama of this scene.

Lorenzo Lotto was one of several Italian painters who created a dramatic new style in the sixteenth century. Recognizing that life itself was often a series of violent and frightening events, he dramatized these aspects to stir the emotions of the viewer.

Annunciation portrays a scene from the New Testament in which the angel Gabriel informs the Virgin Mary that she will become the mother of Christ. Lotto portrayed Mary in a way that was considered shocking in his time. Mary was usually pictured as a symbol of purity and perfection. But his portrait of Mary shows us a real person, swirling away from Gabriel, alarmed by his message. Lotto suggested her motion and unrest in the sweeping folds of her clothes.

The most unusual aspect of this painting is the frightened cat leaping away from the angel. The cat, cherished by ancient cultures as a symbol of fertility and motherhood, came to be identified with pagan rituals and witchcraft as Christianity had taken hold in Europe. It was now viewed as the devil's companion. But Lotto boldly restored the feline to religious painting, and portrayed this tiger cat with careful attention to its leaping form and well-defined features.

THE WHITE CAT, 1817–18
Théodore Géricault, French (1791–1824), Oil on canvas, 15" x 17³/4"

Théodore Géricault first showed his work in 1812 at the Salon—the state-sponsored art exhibition held each year in Paris. The French Empire stretched from Spain to Italy, and Napoléon's army was advancing into Russia that year. Géricault's portrait of a cavalry officer on a rearing horse seemed like a true picture of French heroism. But his bold technique of vivid colors and swirling brush strokes shocked the established artists of the time, whose own paintings had surfaces as smooth as glass. In 1815, Napoléon and the French Empire were defeated at Waterloo. Two years later, Géricault painted this cat to express his belief that France would rise again.

The reclining tomcat shows signs of relaxation—front paw softly tucked under, hind legs gracefully crossed. But his ears are attuned to the sound of an intruder, his wary eye is sharply focused, his tail is about to snap into action. This is an expression of pent-up energy ready to explode.

Géricault created the fresh, silvery tones of the cat's fur by painting directly onto a white canvas with broad areas of white paint. With energetic brush strokes, he shaped the cat's powerful form, using a warm gray color. The plain background and the crescent-shaped shadow focus our attention on the animal. Géricault created the soft-looking fur of the ruff and the ears with brilliant white highlights that overlap the background.

Théodore Géricault said that it was his mission, as an artist, to illuminate and amaze the world with his brilliance. In this painting, he suggested that France, like the cat, had nine lives—and would soon regain its glory.

Théodore Géricault sketched rapidly with a soft pencil to capture this cat's changing expressions and powerful body.

GIRL AND CAT, about 1840
William Thompson Bartoli, American (1817–59), Oil on canvas, 27$\frac{1}{8}$" x 22$\frac{1}{8}$"

*A*merican folk art is a people's art. It was developed by painters who had no formal training but possessed great technical skill. Because their clients were usually plain country people, folk artists did not try to romanticize their subjects. Instead, they created unassuming images of family life.

William Thompson Bartoli began as a sign maker, but soon discovered that he had a gift for painting pictures. Bartoli lived in Marblehead, Massachusetts, where he created portraits of shipbuilders, sea captains, and their families.

In *Girl and Cat,* Bartoli captured the expression of an impatient little girl holding her pet. The cat's blank stare makes us think it has given up hope of escaping her grip. Bartoli created the girl's soft features by forming the shapes with delicate, bluish shadows—picking up the color of her ribbons. He repeated the rich pumpkin color of her dress for the cat's eyes, and warmed the girl's cheeks with a tint of the same color. The intense contrast of a velvety green background enhances the girl's delicate skin tones. Bartoli formed the effect of the cat's fur by blurring the black edges into the orange of the dress.

Bartoli composed this painting in the tradition of American folk portraits—a single figure shown from the knees up, in a simple pose against a plain background. His lack of art school training is noticeable in the clumsily drawn fingers and the oddly shaped cat. But with his talent for expressing this young girl's personality, he set himself apart.

Cornelis Visscher suggests the napping cat's inner alertness through his portrayal of a nervous-looking mouse in the background. Visscher created many overlapping lines to form velvety black and gray tones in the cat's fur.

THE CAT, 1850–1899
Unknown American artist, Oil on canvas, 16" x 20"

The artist who created this painting left no clues behind. The only certainty is that the red bird is a cardinal and the other two are exotic species, either from Latin America or straight from the painter's imagination. This odd portrait invites us to imagine what he or she had in mind.

American folk art paintings were created by self-taught artists. Because these painters were not trained in drawing from models, they often used imagination rather than the close observation of their subject. The results were often more original in concept than the work of highly trained artists.

This painting is composed with humor and contrasts. The cat's head, compared with the trees, is enormous and well defined. A plain, milky blue sky and the dark grass focus our attention on the technical skill of the painter, who created the proud, alert cat in exquisite detail. From the highlights on the glistening eyes to the bristling whiskers, not a brush stroke is out of place. The birds, in comparison, are painted like ornaments decorating the trees. And the little flowers in the background resemble nineteenth-century embroidery patterns.

The artist also created a powerful expression of personality. The cat's intently focused eyes make us think that it is working out a plan. With one bird "in hand," what to do about the two "in the bush"? The artist might have been arguing against the old saying "A bird in the hand is worth two in the bush," which means that possession is better than hope. The successful, professional-looking bird hunter could be a symbol of American know-how: a cat willing to risk losing everything in order to reap great rewards.

Steinlen reveals his wonderful sense of humor in this ink drawing of his cat playing with a goldfish in a bowl.

CAT BATHING, Edo period, Ukiyo-e school, date unknown
Andō Hiroshige, Japanese (1797–1858), Color and ink on paper, 10 15/16" x 7 7/16"

In nineteenth-century Tokyo, then known as Edo, wealthy merchants spared no expense on paintings and decorations for their lavish mansions. They especially liked images of beautiful women wearing elaborate kimonos, often grooming themselves. This art form became known as genre painting—pictures of everyday life.

Andō Hiroshige became a professional artist at the age of fourteen. Like his contemporaries, he also created genre paintings. As Hiroshige became more and more successful, he turned his attention to painting scenes of nature, with flowers, birds, and animals. In this amusing portrait, Hiroshige makes a joke about the frivolous Edo life of pleasure.

A feline so beautiful that she might provoke "catty" remarks from her plainer companions takes a human-style bath. As she sponges her forehead, a kimono slips down to reveal her feminine form. Hiroshige captured the cat's features with a few expressive strokes of *sumi*—black watercolor ink. He diluted the ink into a watery wash for the markings to give the figure its solid form. In painting the robe, Hiroshige let some of the paper show through to create a contrast with the blue ink.

Hiroshige achieved his great skill as a painter by regularly drawing from nature. He was able to create a perfect expression of any subject with a few, well-observed lines. In painting with ink on paper, an artist must be absolutely sure of himself, for he cannot erase or cover his mistakes. In *Cat Bathing*, Hiroshige shows his genius—and his sly sense of humor.

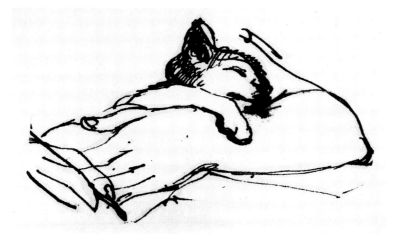

Jean-Auguste-Dominique Ingres (1780–1867) was known for his formal portraits of important people. In this informal drawing, Ingres sketched few lines to portray a contented kitten asleep in his wife's arms.

18

CHESHIRE CAT, 1865
Sir John Tenniel, English (1820–1914), Wood engraving, 3 $^9/_{16}$" x 2 $^{13}/_{16}$"

Sir John Tenniel studied painting at the Royal Academy of Art in London. But he had a gift for creating illustrations—drawings that enhance the meaning of a story. For *Alice's Adventures in Wonderland,* a book by Lewis Carroll, Tenniel created a timeless cast of characters.

One of these fantastical creatures is the grinning Cheshire Cat, who could vanish into thin air. It was he who explained to Alice that in Wonderland, everybody was crazy. The cat appeared at a croquet match held by the King and Queen of Hearts, and the Queen was greatly annoyed by his lack of respect. "Off with his head!" she shouted. The clever cat began to disappear, until all that remained was his face. Tenniel's illustration depicts a mad debate between the King, the Queen, and the executioner on how to behead a creature without a body.

Tenniel worked from his imagination to draw these characters. He gave life to the playing-card figures of the King and Queen by exaggerating their features. The faces are large and simply drawn—in contrast to their clothes, which are patterned with overall designs. Tenniel drew the Cheshire Cat's face with an almost human expression. His enormous size, compared with that of the other figures, makes the cat's importance immediately clear.

Tenniel balanced the white areas in this drawing—the faces, and the costumes of the King and the executioner—with shading that consists of overlapping lines. With this *hatching* technique, Tenniel created many shades of gray.

Success as an illustrator of books and as a cartoonist for the weekly magazine *Punch* left Tenniel little time for painting. He occasionally exhibited watercolor paintings, but the more than 2,500 illustrations he created in his lifetime earned him a knighthood in 1893.

Rudyard Kipling (1865–1936), an English author, created this illustration for his story "The Cat That Walked by Himself." The steep angle of the alley of trees, the stark contrast of black and white, and the cat's proudly snapping tail speak of its independence from people who wish to tame it.

WOMAN WITH CAT, about 1875
Pierre-Auguste Renoir, French (1841–1919), Oil on canvas, 22" x 18¼"

When your best friend is a cat, your most important secrets will be safe. Pierre-Auguste Renoir captured an intimate conversation between a young woman and her pet in this delicate portrait.

Renoir took a close view of his subjects and displayed his gift for painting the woman's luminous skin, the texture of her silky hair, and the cat's luxurious coat. He used a range of quiet colors—delicate rose, golden brown, and celadon green. To create pearly skin tones, Renoir diluted the paint with linseed oil and turpentine and applied it in thin layers. He mixed the rose tints of the woman's cheeks and fingers directly into the wet ivory color he had previously applied to the canvas. In the same way, he added rosy highlights to the auburn color of her hair.

Renoir applied thicker layers of color for the cat, and used stiff bristle brushes to lift up furry-looking textures in the wet paint. He formed the effect of the fluffy ruff and the whispers of fur in the ears with touches of opaque white paint. Renoir captured the cat's relaxed little paws with the same delicacy as he did the woman's graceful fingers.

The soft green background is important to the warm effect that Renoir achieved in this portrait. He used a canvas that was covered with a cream-colored base coat, called a *ground*. Renoir applied the green paint in a thin layer, letting the yellowish ground show through. He repeated the green color in darker and lighter tones on the upholstery, on the curtains, and on the woman's ring to unite the background with the subjects—and create a feeling of closeness.

Wilhelm Busch (1832–1908), the beloved children's-book author, also created illustrations for his stories. In these drawings from his personal sketchbook, he studied the soft form and expression of two sleeping kittens.

TINKLE, A CAT, 1883
Unknown American artist, Oil on academy board, 23¾" x 18"

All that is known about this painting is that Tinkle was two years and two months old when she sat for her portrait. In traditional American folk art, pets were usually portrayed with their owners. But we must use our imagination to picture the loving owner who wished this adored cat to be remembered.

Tinkle sits on an elegant velvet hassock trimmed with black and gold braid. On her collar, two golden bells, which would ring out a warning as she moves, might make us think she was a ferocious bird hunter. The solid black background creates a striking contrast to the white cat—and an air of formality.

It is well known that all cats, even the most independent ones, have the ability to strike the pose of a perfect, well-behaved animal. The artist captured typical feline qualities in this painting, making Tinkle a symbol of her species. Tinkle rises to full height, with her tail completely still. Her alert ears are painted a pearly pink, to proclaim the cat's cleanliness. Her greenish yellow eyes, emphasized by the black pupils, seem alive. The whiskers, nearly invisible against her white fur, are indicated with little black dots below the nose.

The unknown artist painted in a straightforward style. A few shadows define Tinkle's chin, legs, and tail. The painter created the soft effect of fur by blurring the edges of the cat with a nearly dry white paint and letting the background colors show through. The simplicity of the composition and the clear expression of Tinkle's character make a lasting impression.

Théophile-Alexandre Steinlen (1859-1923) became famous for his drawings and paintings of cats. Here, he studied his cat in various positions of complete relaxation.

MAN WITH THE CAT, 1898
Cecilia Beaux, American (1863–1942), Oil on canvas, 48" x 34⅝"

Cecilia Beaux was raised in Philadelphia by her aunts after the death of her mother. Katherine Ann Drinker, a well-known painter, took charge of Cecilia's education. At the age of fifteen, Beaux decided to become a professional artist. Later, in 1888, she moved to Paris and studied at the Academy Julien. After two years, Beaux returned to Philadelphia and established her reputation as a portrait painter. In 1895, she became the first full-time woman teacher at the Pennsylvania Academy of Fine Arts.

The "man with the cat" was Beaux's brother-in-law, Henry Sturgis Drinker — a distinguished attorney for the Lehigh Valley Railroad who also specialized in forest management. Beaux captured Drinker's dignity and his affection for an orange calico cat that clearly enjoys having its toes stroked.

Beaux created the effect of sunlight playing on pale surfaces with energetic brush strokes. She painted Drinker's face with bold patches of color and added just enough detail to define his features. The shadows on his face add an air of sadness, in contrast to the bright light. Beaux captured the essence of relaxation in the cat's facial expression. To form the soft texture of its fur, she feathered in an ivory glaze over the underlying orange shape, using small brushes. Beaux suggested a luxurious living room with large blocks of pale gray, cream, and rose.

During her lifetime, Cecilia Beaux was recognized as one of the great American portrait painters, and a retrospective exhibition in 1974 brought new appreciation for her work.

Jean-Baptiste Oudry (1686–1755) crowded the two kittens up to the edges of this gouache painting to dramatize their actions.

FLOWERS AND CATS, 1889
Paul Gauguin, French (1848–1903), Oil on canvas, 36³/4" x 28³/8"

*E*ighteen eighty-nine was an exciting year in Paris. The Eiffel Tower was finished and the Paris World's Fair opened. There, Paul Gauguin organized a large exhibition; he hoped to sell enough paintings to support himself. But it was a failure and he was running out of money. Gauguin moved to the small village of Le Pouldu, stayed with an artist friend who paid the rent, and painted. He also filled his sketchbook with drawings of the landlord's cats.

Artists often choose to paint still life because they can move objects around until they have an arrangement they like. In this painting, Gauguin portrayed these two kittens more as objects than as living things—they look very much like the statues that he sculpted from clay. He exaggerated the waking cat's features with bold, dark outlines to give it a strong presence next to the towering bouquet of flowers. Gauguin painted the sleeping cat's calico markings in wedges of yellow, orange, and brown. He separated this cat from the dark background with a few bristling strokes of white paint.

Gauguin painted the flowers in an explosion of color. He outlined the pale blossoms to define their details, but shaped the red flowers with color alone. Gauguin left plenty of "empty space" at the edges of the bouquet to give the arrangement form. He painted a thin wash of pink over a lavender background, letting the lavender show through—creating a soft tone that echoes the colors in the bouquet. The two cats are like statues carefully positioned on the dark tabletop to balance the composition.

Mary Cassatt (1845–1926) created inky, dark tones in this portrait by making crisscross marks, which are known as hatching.

WOMAN WITH A CAT, 1912

Pierre Bonnard, French (1867–1947), Oil on canvas, 30¾" x 30¼"

Pierre Bonnard found charm and gaiety in everyday events. He was a keen observer who painted from memory to express his feeling for special moments in his life. Bonnard believed that if he painted using models, the details of the model and the surroundings would distract him from the images stored in his mind.

Bonnard's cat was an important member of the family and is the featured subject of this painting. As his wife, Marthe, intently listens to a conversation, kitty prepares to pounce. Bonnard captured the cat's intense concentration as it pauses, keeping an eye on Madame Bonnard, ready to snatch the little fish from her plate.

Bonnard used sharply contrasting colors—red, blue, and white—to make the cat the most important figure in this painting. He "framed" the tall white animal between the fireplace at the right and the window frame at the left to focus our attention on this humorous scene. Madame Bonnard's face and hair are painted in rosy colors that almost blend in with the wall behind her, in contrast to the bold presence of her feline dinner companion.

The room glistens with sunlight; the table-cloth is warmed with dabs of yellow paint; the plums and the crystal bowl shimmer with white highlights. The only shadows are formed by the pale lavender shapes next to the bowl and on the rumpled napkins in the foreground.

Bonnard said, "I would like to land before the young people, in the year 2000, with the wings of a butterfly." His pictures of blissful family life, like this one with his wife and their cat, bring his vision of happiness to us today.

With keen observation and a sure hand, Bonnard captured a tabby in deep thought, using ink and a nearly dry brush.

PARIS THROUGH THE WINDOW, 1913
Marc Chagall, Russian (1887–1985), Oil on canvas, 53$\frac{1}{2}$" x 55$\frac{3}{4}$"

Marc Chagall dreamed of living in the greatest center of art—Paris. In 1910, he left his native Russia for the "City of Light," where he found excitement everywhere—in the street markets, the cafés, the art galleries and museums. At first, Chagall was homesick. But he was inspired by the vitality of the international city and the work of contemporary painters. Chagall soon felt at home, and he unlocked his vision in the fantastical paintings he began to create.

Paris Through the Window was Chagall's tribute to the city where he was reborn as an artist. It seems like a dream that has come to life, with a shimmering Eiffel Tower, people floating magically through the air, and a little train that travels upside down. The two-headed man is Chagall himself—looking forward to an exciting future but also looking back to Russia and to his fiancée there, whom he desperately missed. On the windowsill, a mysterious cat with a human face seems to be talking with the artist. This imaginary animal expresses the happiness Chagall felt when his paintings were first recognized by the public as great works of art.

The window, with its red, yellow, blue, and green frame, opens onto a world where Chagall had seen everyday events take on a new spirit, when he looked with "the eyes of his soul." Chagall depicted the light of Paris as silvery pyramids that illuminate the painting. With intense, joyous colors, he revealed secret images that only he could see.

In 1914, Chagall had his first one-man exhibition in Berlin. On the wings of success, he returned to Russia for a happy reunion with his future wife, Bella Rosenfeld.

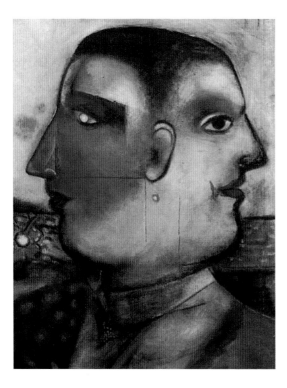

With sparkling colors as clear as a stained-glass window, Chagall created a self-portrait. He looks forward to a successful future, and back to his native Russian roots.

TWO CATS, 1913
Franz Marc, German (1880–1916), Oil on canvas, 29" x 35½"

At the turn of the century, Germany experienced rapid industrial growth, and many of its people became obsessed with power and money. Franz Marc was depressed by the greed that surrounded him, and searched for the meaning of life in nature. He believed that animals had a special, innocent power that humans could not spoil. Marc created a visual language, using colors and shapes to express his idea of the natural strength, courage, and goodness of animals.

The two cats in this painting are occupied with the usual feline activities. The blue cat is busily washing itself, and the yellow cat is coiled up, ready to attack. At first, it seems that the yellow cat is fixed on a toy—the green ball. But we soon notice that a red mouse in the foreground is the target. Franz Marc used color to express the animals' characteristics. Blue was a male color, representing strength; yellow, a female color, for sensuality; red meant aggression. By mixing colors to create new shades, he changed the meaning of the original colors. For example, he mixed red and yellow to create a patch of orange, which expresses the yellow cat's fierceness. Marc painted circular forms on the shoulder and hindquarters of the blue cat to emphasize its strong muscles—suggesting that this one is a fighter. He outlined the yellow cat's features in black and gray to portray its intense concentration.

These two cats occupy a primitive landscape, which Marc painted in bold patterns and intense colors. With the little white house in the background, he hints at the remote—and unnecessary—presence of people.

Alexander Calder (1898–1976), an American sculptor loved for his whimsical circus figures, made this ink drawing of a sly cat cleaning itself. He drew one nearly continuous line—leaving blank spaces for the imagination to complete.

CAT AND BIRD, 1928
Paul Klee, German (1879–1940), Oil and ink on canvas mounted on wood, 15" x 21"

*P*aul Klee's studio was called "The Wizard's Kitchen" by his friend, the painter Lothar Schreyer. Enveloped in a small blue cloud of smoke rising from his pipe, Klee was surrounded by a clutter of brushes, scrapers, paints, bottles, chalks, paper, and easels. From this chaotic assortment of materials sprang paintings, drawings, and sculpture that seem like visions created by a sorcerer—of a world somewhere between dreams and reality.

One of Klee's companions was Fritzi, a tiger tomcat with wildcat blood. Fritzi was not completely tame, but he was always forgiven when he knocked things over in the crowded studio. His powerful hunting instinct was Klee's inspiration for *Cat and Bird*.

Klee created an image that seems more like a primitive mask than a portrait. He exaggerated the size of the eyes to represent the extraordinary vision of cats. Two arcs above the eyes describe the concentration typical of the hunting feline. The heart-shaped nose represents Klee's affection for Fritzi's independent nature.

A narrow range of reds, earth colors, and greens, along with white and black, gives this close-up "portrait" great warmth and intensity. Klee formed the image and background in thick patches of color. While the paint was wet, he scratched in the outlines, which he filled with ink after the paint had dried.

Paul Klee often used animal images to express his vision of nature's extremes. He said that it was probably true that only children, madmen, and primitives could understand the mischievous dream world that he created in his paintings.

At the age of fifteen, Klee's son Felix sketched Fritzi, the household pet. With a few marks, he drew an almost human expression on the favorite cat's sleeping face.

CAT SEIZING BIRD, 1939
Pablo Picasso, Spanish (1881–1973), Oil on canvas, 31 7/8" x 39 1/4"

In the spring of 1939, Europe faced the darkest years in modern history. The Nazi German dictator Adolf Hitler had already seized Austria and Czechoslovakia. He now threatened to gobble up Poland. Pablo Picasso recognized Hitler's hunger for power, and he created this powerful image as a warning.

In *Cat Seizing Bird,* Picasso identified the mad dictator as a sinister cat destroying the dove of peace. The predatory cat grips the earth in his razorlike talons; the bulging stomach shows his greed. The face seems like a nightmare come to life, with one eye on the helpless bird, the other staring blankly at the future.

Picasso created a feeling of anxiety through his use of line, form, and color. He drew the cat's head in a simplified shape that resembles a primitive demon mask. The neck and legs are sharp and angular; the cat's arched back and stiff tail express rigid determination. The animal dominates the space of the canvas, just as Hitler would soon dominate Europe. Picasso used dark and cold colors—greenish black, gray, and brown—to focus our attention on the fiendish beast. He painted a few white outlines on the cat to emphasize the sharp angles and to separate it from the background.

Five months after Picasso signed this painting, France and England declared war on Germany. As a Spanish citizen, Picasso was not called to military service. He remained in France throughout the German occupation and used his paints and brushes as weapons of protest in the struggle for peace.

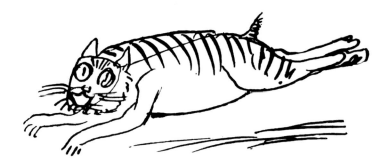

Edward Lear (1812–88), an English painter and author of The Owl and the Pussycat, *made this nonsensical ink drawing of his cat, Foss, in pursuit of big game.*

THE CHESS GAME, 1956
George Tooker, American (born 1920), Tempera on a panel, 30" x 15"

George Tooker is fascinated by the dramatic style of sixteenth-century Italian painting. Like Lorenzo Lotto (p. 11), Tooker created an electrifying scene to portray an important event—his decision to become a full- time artist.

The Chess Game is a symbolic self-portrait in which the game stands for the financial success Tooker will give up as he struggles to achieve success as a painter. We can see that he is losing—Tooker has only two white pieces left on the board. The young woman who is winning holds up a red game piece in a teasing way. Tooker stands back from the table as a spitting cat lunges at his ankles.

The tall, narrow shape of the painting and the repetition of geometric patterns make the room seem crowded. The square table and a chess board set at a dizzying angle repeat the checkered floor pattern. A room in the back is softened into a spooky mist, making it seem far away. From behind the glass, two neighbors look on in alarm. Icy tones of black, white, and gray—repeated throughout—appear even colder, in contrast to the woman's bright red skirt.

Tooker created the tunnel-like effect in the picture by using the *perspective drawing* technique. High ceilings, steep angles, and a series of doors and windows make the space appear to rush toward the background. The checkerboard floor tilts dangerously forward and Tooker seems to be losing his footing.

George Tooker followed his desire to be an artist at a time when realistic painting was overlooked in favor of abstract art. For ten years, Tooker built furniture to earn money. Today, his work is collected by patrons who appreciate paintings that tell of the difficulties in modern life.

Using fine brushes, Tooker shaped the cat's lean, muscular body with gradual shadows. The white highlights on its black eyes focus our attention on the snarling face.

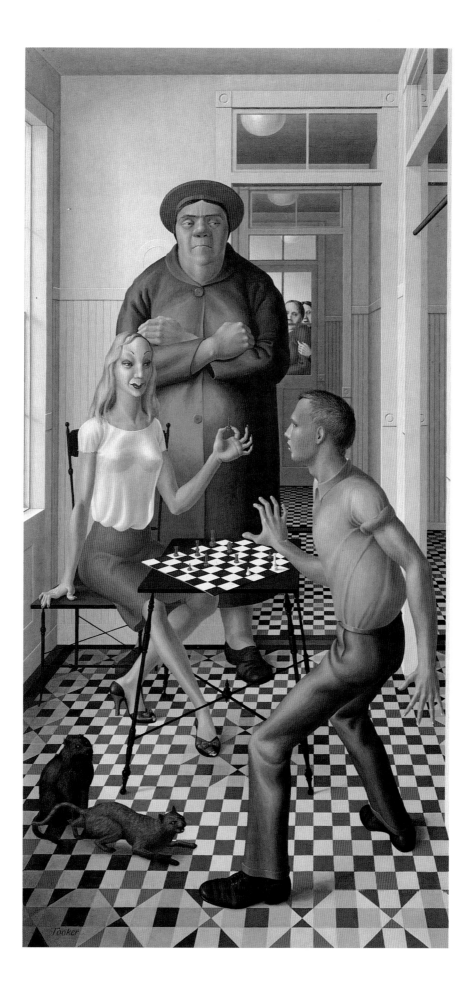

WOMAN AND CATS, 1962
Will Barnet, American (born 1911), Oil on canvas, 45" x 50"

Will Barnet observed his graceful wife, Elena, as she lifted their cat, Madame Butterfly, into her arms. Barnet was inspired by the curves of Elena's body—echoed by those of the supple feline—to create this dreamlike portrait.

Before he began to paint, Barnet filled four sketchbooks with drawings of Elena and the cat. Through keen observation, he discovered the hidden forms that portrayed her strength and the cat's fluidness. He redrew these images from memory to express their essential character. As Barnet shaped the picture, he decided that two cats would make a more pleasing composition.

Barnet conveyed a serene mood through the carefully designed empty spaces. The gray background covers about the same area as the figures, giving the painting visual balance. Two wedges of gray separate the figure from the edges to suggest a roomy space. Barnet also painted a few straight lines in contrast to the many curves.

At first, it seems that Elena's robe is a flat color, almost like a silhouette. Looking closely, we can see that Barnet painted a thin layer of orange paint over yellow, which shows through. Delicate touches of gray give solidity to the precisely defined shapes. Elena's skin tones are built up with translucent ivory paint over a rose color. In contrast, the two cats are solid black.

Madame Butterfly selected the Barnets as her human companions. One day, she scratched on their screen door to announce her arrival, promptly moved in, and spent fifteen happy years as the artist's model and cherished family pet.

Will Barnet used a greasy crayon to form the soft textures of the cat's fur. The white background focuses our attention on the sweeping curves of the cat.

MR. AND MRS. CLARK AND PERCY, 1970–71
David Hockney, English (born 1937), Acrylic on canvas, 84" x 120"

London in the 1960s was the youth capital of the world. The Beatles and the Rolling Stones created a new sound in popular music, and the "mod" look in fashion was adopted from New York to Tokyo. The worlds of film, music, fashion, and art exploded into a new global culture, led by talented young artists from the working class.

Ossie Clark and Celia Birtwell—fashion and textile designers—created trendy clothes that were worn by young aristocrats and rock groups. When they were married in 1969, David Hockney—Ossie's close friend from art school—created this portrait as a wedding portrait.

Hockney filled the painting with historical and contemporary symbolic images. White lilies, which have represented a woman's chastity since biblical times, sit on a modern table. The white cat, Percy, stands in as a symbol for fidelity—inspired by a little dog in *The Betrothal of the Arnolfini,* painted by Jan van Eyck in 1434. A telephone next to the chair sits ready to electronically connect the couple to the entire world, and the sparse furnishings suggest a life spent in jet airplanes rather than at home.

This portrait seems so real we almost feel we have intruded on the Clarks, who have just awakened. Hockney painted the nearly life-size figures and the setting in photo-realistic detail. The light slanting in through the partly shuttered window creates contrasting highlights and shadows on the Clarks' faces and casts Percy in sharp relief. Hockney painted every strand of the shag rug, but softened the garden and the distant building seen through the window.

Franz Kline (1910–62), an American painter known for his powerful black-and-white images, drew Kitska's sleek curves and soft fur with rapid brush strokes of black ink.

Glossary and Index

ABSTRACT, 40: Having form and color, but not recognizable subject matter.

Annunciation, 11

ARCHAEOLOGIST, 8: One who studies the culture and life of the past by unearthing and studying ruins, and objects found in ruins.

BACKGROUND, 8, 12: The part of a painting behind the subject; the distant area. (See FOREGROUND.)

Barnet, Will, 42

Bartoli, William Thompson, 14

Beaux, Cecilia, 26 (Pronounced Sih-seal-yuh Boh)

Bonnard, Pierre, 30

CANVAS, 12, 22, 38: A woven fabric (often linen or cotton) used as a painting surface. It is usually stretched tight and stapled onto a wooden frame in order to produce a flat, unwrinkled surface.

Cat, The, 16

Cat and Bird, 36

Cat Bathing, 18

Cat Seizing Bird, 38

Chagall, Marc, 32

Cheshire Cat, 20

Chess Game, The, 40

COMPOSITION, CONTRAST, 8, 14, 16, 18, 20, 22, 24, 26, 30, 40, 42, 44: Big differences in light and dark, shapes, colors, and activity.

DESIGN, 20, 42: (1) The arrangement of objects and figures in a painting through the combination of colors and shapes. This is also called composition. (2) A pattern of shapes on a surface.

DETAIL, 10, 16, 26, 28, 30, 44: (1) Small parts of a painting, such as objects on a table or decorations on a dress. (2) When used in a book: a section of a painting enlarged to provide a close-up view of textures and colors.

DRAWING, 10, 16, 18, 20, 22, 28, 36, 40, 42: The art of creating an image by making marks on paper. Drawings can be made using dry materials such as pencil, charcoal, and crayon or wet materials such as ink and paint. Drawings may consist of lines, tones, shading, and dots. Twentieth-century artists began to create drawings that are difficult to distinguish from paintings. An important difference is that drawings are usually on paper rather than on canvas, wood, or metal. Drawings produced with more than one kind of material are known as "mixed media" drawings.

FACSIMILE PAINTING, 8 (Pronounced fak-sim-uh-lee): An exact copy.

Flowers and Cats, 28

FOREGROUND, 30, 34: The area in a painting closest to the viewer. (See BACKGROUND.)

Gauguin, Paul, 28 (Pronounced Go-gann)

GENRE PAINTING, 18: Pictures that depict everyday life or everyday events in a realistic way.

Géricault, Théodore, 12 (Pronounced Tay-a-door Zher-ih-koh)

Girl and Cat, 14

GLAZE, 26: A transparent, or almost transparent, thinned-down layer of paint applied over dry paint, allowing the colors underneath to show through.

GROUND, 22: A coating applied to a painting surface to create an even texture.

HATCHING, 20: Fine lines drawn closely together to create shading.

HIGHLIGHT, 12, 16, 22, 30, 44: The lightest color or brightest white in a painting.

Hiroshige, Andō, 18 (Pronounced An-doh Her-oh-shih-guh)

Hockney, David, 44

ILLUSTRATION, 20: A drawing or painting created to enhance the meaning of a text in books, magazines, posters, and newspapers.

ILLUSTRATOR, 20: An artist who creates illustrations.

INK, 28, 36: Usually, a jet-black fluid made of powdered carbon mixed with a water-soluble liquid. Ink drawings can be made with dark lines and diluted tones of gray. Inks are also made in colors and used in paintings.

Klee, Paul, 36

LINE, 18, 20, 38, 42: A mark, such as a pencil mark, that does not include gradual shades or tones.

Lotto, Lorenzo, 10, 40

Man with the Cat, 26

Marc, Franz, 34

Mr. and Mrs. Clark and Percy, 44

OPAQUE, 22: Not letting light pass through. Opaque paints conceal what is under them. (The opposite of TRANSPARENT.)

PAINT: Artists have used different kinds of paint, depending on the materials that were available to them and the effects they wished to produce in their work.

Different kinds of paint are similar in the way they are made.

1. Paint is made by combining finely powdered pigment with a vehicle. A vehicle is a substance that evenly disperses the color and produces a consistency that can be like mayonnaise and sometimes as thick as peanut butter. The kind of vehicle used sometimes gives the paint its name. Pigment is the raw material that gives paint its color. Pigments are made from natural minerals and from man-made chemical compounds.

2. Paint is made thinner or thicker with a substance called a medium. Different paints require the use of mediums appropriate to their composition.

3. A solvent must be used by the painter to clean the paint from brushes, tools, and the hands. The solvent must be appropriate for the composition of the paint.

ACRYLIC PAINT: Pigment is combined with an acrylic polymervehicle that is created in a laboratory. By itself, acrylic paint dries rapidly. Several different mediums can be used with acrylic paint: Retarders slow the drying process, flow extenders thin the paint, an impasto medium thickens the paint, a gloss medium makes it shiny, a matte medium makes it dull.

Acrylic paint has been popular since the 1960s. Many artists like its versatility and the wide range of colors. Acrylic paint is also appreciated because its solvent is water, which is nonhazardous.

OIL PAINT, 10, 22: Pigment is combined with an oil vehicle (usually linseed or poppy oil). The medium chosen by most artists is linseed oil. The solvent is turpentine. Oil paint dries slowly, which enables the artist to work on a painting for a long time. Some painters mix other materials, such as pumice or marble dust, into oil paint to produce thick layers of color. Oil paint is never mixed with water. Oil paint has been used since the fifteenth century. Until the early nineteenth century, artists or their assistants ground the pigment and combined the ingredients of paint in their studios. In 1840, paint became available in flexible tin tubes (like toothpaste tubes).

TEMPERA, 40: Pigment is combined with a water-based vehicle. The paint is combined with raw egg yolk to "temper" it into a mayonnaiselike consistency usable with a brush. The solvent for tempera is water. Tempera was used by the ancient Greeks and was the favorite method of painters during the medieval period in Europe. It is now available in tubes, ready to use. The painter supplies the egg yolk.

WATERCOLOR, 18, 20: Pigment is combined with gum arabic, a water-based vehicle. Water is both the medium and the solvent. Watercolor paint now comes ready to use in tubes (moist) or in cakes (dry). With transparent watercolor, unlike other painting techniques, white paint is not used to lighten the colors. Watercolor paint is thinned with water, and areas of paper are often left uncovered to produce highlights. Watercolor paint was first used 37,000 years ago by cave dwellers who created the first wall paintings.

GOUACHE: An opaque form of watercolor. Also called tempera.

Paris Through the Window, 32

PATRON, 40: An individual who supports the arts or an individual artist.

PERSPECTIVE, 10, 40: A method of representing people, places, and things in a painting or drawing to make them appear solid or three-dimensional rather than flat. Six basic rules of perspective are used in Western art.

1. People in a painting appear larger when near and gradually become smaller as they get farther away.

2. People in the foreground overlap the activity behind them.

3. People become closer together as they get farther away.

4. People in the distance appear higher up in the picture than those in the foreground.

5. Colors are brighter and shadows are stronger in the foreground. Colors and shadows are paler and softer in the background. This effect is also called *aerial perspective*.

6. Lines that, in real life, are parallel (such as the line of a ceiling and the line of a floor) are drawn at an angle, and the lines meet at the "horizon line," which represents the eye level of the viewer.

Painters have used these methods to depict objects in space since the fifteenth century. But many twentieth-century artists do not use perspective. An artist might emphasize color, line, or shape to express an idea, instead of depicting a realistic space.

Picasso, Pablo, 38

PORTRAIT, 10, 12, 14, 16, 18, 22, 24, 26, 36, 42, 44: A painting, drawing, sculpture, or photograph that represents an individual's appearance and, often, his or her personality.

Renoir, Pierre-Auguste, 22 (Pronounced Rehn-wahr)

SELF-PORTRAIT, 40: A portrait of the artist created by the artist.

SHADING, 18: The use of gradually darker and lighter colors to make an object appear solid and three-dimensional.

SHADOW, 12, 14, 24, 26, 30, 44: An area made darker than its surroundings because the light has been cut off by an object between the light and the area in shadow.

SILHOUETTE, 8, 42: An image, such as a portrait or an object, that consists of the outline of its shape, in a solid color.

SKETCH, 20, 22, 24, 28, 36, 42: A quickly made drawing.

STILL LIFE, 28: A painting, drawing or photograph of an object, or a group of objects.

Sun God Ra in the Form of a Cat, The, 8

Tenniel, Sir John, 18

TEXTURE, 26, 42: The surface quality of a painting. For example, an oil painting could have a thin, smooth surface texture, or a thick, rough surface texture.

Tinkle, a Cat, 15

TONE, 12, 14, 22, 28, 40, 42: The sensation of an overall coloration in a painting. For example, an artist might begin by painting the entire picture in shades of greenish gray. After more colors are applied using transparent glazes, shadows, and highlights, the mass of greenish gray color underneath will show through and create an even tone, or "tonal harmony."

Tooker, George, 40

TRANSPARENT: Allowing light to pass through so colors underneath can be seen. (The opposite of OPAQUE.)

TURPENTINE, 22: A strong-smelling solvent made from pine sap; used in oil painting. (See PAINT: OIL PAINT.)

Two Cats, 34

Unknown American artist, 14, 16

White Cat, The, 12
Woman and Cats, 42
Woman with a Cat, 30
Woman with Cat, 22

Credits